LEARN FRENCH THE NAUGHTY WAY

REAL-LIFE FRENCH SLANG AND SWEAR WORDS YOU DON'T LEARN IN THE CLASSROOM

FRENCH HACKING

Copyright © 2024 French Hacking

All rights reserved. No part of this publication may be reproduced, distributed or transmitted in any form or by any means, including photocopying, recording, or other electronic or mechanical methods, without the prior written permission of the publisher, except in the case of brief quotations embodied in critical reviews and certain other non-commercial uses permitted by copyright law.

Trademarked names appear throughout this book. Rather than use a trademark symbol with every occurrence of a trademarked name, names are used in an editorial fashion, with no intention of infringement of the respective owner's trademark. The information in this book is distributed on an "as is" basis, without warranty. Although every precaution has been taken in the preparation of this work, neither the author nor the publisher shall have any liability to any person or entity with respect to any loss or damage caused or alleged to be caused directly or indirectly by the information contained in this book.

"One language sets you in a corridor for life. Two languages open every door along the way."

— Frank Smith

French Hacking

French Hacking is a revolutionary educational language learning company focused on teaching individuals how to learn French in the shortest time possible. Our mission is for our students to develop a command of the French language by utilizing the hacks, tips, and tricks included in the learning materials we create. We want our students to become confident in their speaking abilities as they advance their conversational skills by teaching what's necessary without having to learn the finer details that don't make much of a difference or aren't even used in the real world.

Unlike our competitors, who have books geared toward multiple languages, our language learning books are dedicated exclusively to learning French. Our focus on only one language allows us to truly concentrate on creating superior educational materials.

Our books are created by native French speakers and then put through a vigorous editing process with two more native French editors and proofreaders to ensure the highest quality content. Rest assured that you are learning proper grammar and syntax as you read through our books.

There are no other books like ours on the market. Let us help accelerate your journey to learn French with our fun and effective educational materials that make learning French a breeze!

About this book

This book takes you on a wild ride through the colorful and unfiltered side of the French language. Forget the classroom rules and grammar drills—here, you'll dive into the dirty, naughty, and raw slang and street French that you won't find in textbooks. Packed with authentic expressions and real-life examples, this guide gives you the tools to speak like a true local, whether you're navigating the nightlife, engaging in playful banter, or just aiming to sound cool. Get ready to master the art of French slang with humor and flair!

Who's it for?

This book is designed for those who already have an intermediate knowledge of French and wish to sound more like locals.

BONUS!

Enhance your learning experience by downloading the free audiobook and PDF version of this book. For more details, please refer to the last page. Enjoy learning and exploring these valuable resources at your convenience!

CONTENTS

Using the Book: Pronouncing French   ix
Introduction: A Brief History of French Slang   xiii

1. Greetings & Salutations!   1
2. Everyday Interactions   10
3. Food Fixation   19
4. All About Culture   28
5. The Wrong Side of the Law   39
6. The French Look   46
7. Style Over Substance?   55
8. The Daily French Life   61
9. Matters of Life & Death   68
10. Emotion Explosion   75
11. Money, Money, Money   81
12. Drinking, Dancing, Puking   85
13. Looking for Trouble, Keeping the Peace   97
14. Love Language   107
15. Intercourse   114

USING THE BOOK: PRONOUNCING FRENCH

If your French class experience was mostly daydreaming about Mireille from those old "French in Action" videos, this book might be challenging for you. French slang assumes you already know some French. This is a slang book, and slang is usually learned after basic phrases like "I live in the red house" or "Yes, I like the library very much, thank you." So, this isn't a beginner's grammar book. It's meant to take your French to the next level.

The chapters and explanations are designed so that even with just a little French knowledge, you should be able to handle anyone who starts annoying you with some Merlot-fueled conspiracy theories. You'll find all the slang you need here, organized by subject, chapter after chapter.

The slang is up to date and is the kind you'd hear on the streets of Paris today. Usually, the English is given first, followed by the French, and sometimes the French has alternatives for gender differences. This isn't a grammar book, and you're smart enough to figure it out.

So, before we delve into it, here's a quick refresher on pronouncing *le français*. This isn't about naming the letters of the alphabet but how to pronounce them in words.

    A, à = ah
    B = bay
    C = kah (before "a, o, u"), say (before "e, i")
    Ç = say

D = day
E, è = euh (like the second "e" in "telephone")
É = ay
F = eff
G = gg (before "a, o, u"), zhee (before "e, i")
H = [silent]
I = ee
J = zhay
K = kah
L = elle
M = emm
N = enn
0, ô = oh
P = pay
Q = keww
R = air
S = esse
T = tay
U = eww (shape your mouth like a chicken's asshole — and you'll say it right)
V = vay
X = eeks
Y = ee
Z = z
Je = zheuh (like the "ge" in "garage")
Tu = tew
Il, ils = eel (they're pronounced exactly the same; context is what let's people know when it's plural)
Elle, elles = elle (you might want to check the explanation right above)
On = ohhhn
Nous = nou
Vous = voo (like "voodoo")

The hardest thing for Americans to pronounce in French is the vowels. This is because Americans often speak in monotones and aren't used to emphasizing words differently. To improve your French pronunciation, try speaking with a dramatic French accent, like *Inspector Clouseau*: "Hey dude, ya wanna go get high?" becomes "hAAY dewwwd, yoooo waaahn too gooo geeet hiiii?" Don't worry, you'll get it with practice.

Remember: Slang is situational, and the slang in this book can be intense. Using it at the wrong time or place could get you into trouble. So, only use these expressions with people your age and in situations where you understand what's happening.

Now take your French slang and have fun with it!

INTRODUCTION: A BRIEF HISTORY OF FRENCH SLANG

French slang didn't develop overnight. Over the course of nearly 2,000 years, French evolved from Latin. When the Romans colonized France in the first century BC, their language changed as they interacted with the local Celtic tribes. By the fifth century, after the fall of the Roman Empire, the Latin spoken in France (then called Gaul) had diverged from the Latin spoken in Rome, leading to the birth of the French language. Several more recent factors have contributed to the evolution of formal French into what we now call French slang.

France's colonial empire, known as la Métropole, was second only to the British Empire. The French sent colonists and prisoners to new territories. From these regions, they brought back items like sugar cane, coffee, exotic fruits, latex, rubber, gas, and minerals. While some French people believed it was a win-win situation, as they brought education, hygiene, and democracy to the colonies, the colonial subjects (and their descendants) might have disagreed...

Colonialism greatly influenced French slang. Mixed marriages and hybrid cultures introduced African, Asian, and especially North African Arabic words into French. During colonization, knowledge and language were exchanged between the colonists and the colonies. After the French left their colonies, the returning colonists brought back a new cultural and linguistic identity. Their new vocabulary gradually spread across France, becoming a significant part of the language today.

Finally, English has also made its mark on France – even though the French hate to admit it. Many terms, especially those related to technology and drugs, aren't Frenchified. They keep their English spellings but are pronounced with a French accent. Examples include:

le barbeque, le best-seller, le blues, le bluff, le business, le chewing-gum, le club, le cocktail, le fast-food, le feedback, le freezer, le gangster, l'interview, le joker, le kidnapping, le kit, le leader, le look, le manager, les news, le parking, le pickpocket, le puzzle, se relaxer, le self-service, le software, le snack, le steak, and *le week-end.*

- **VERLAN**

Similar to English Pig Latin, verlan is a way of altering French words.

Unlike Pig Latin, though, verlan is everywhere in French. Turn on the TV, flip through a newspaper, or listen to a song, and you'll hear it. Verlan is commonly used by suburban youth (remember, in France, the suburbs are often ghettos) and has been popularized by the hip-hop scene. But it's not just for youth — housewives, rich kids, and businessmen use it too. They might not speak it fluently, but you'll hear them use plenty of verlan words!

Verlan changes French words, including slang and foreign words, and creates new ones by switching syllables or reading them backward. That's why it's called verlan (from *l'envers,* which means backward). Sometimes, other transformations occur such as the shortening of the base words. This book will teach you some verlan techniques to help you understand what's coming up in the next chapters.

Verlan is made in several different ways. The first example is for words with two or three syllables. The syllables are switched, placing the second syllable in first position:

    barbu → **bubart**: bearded
    arnaque → **carna**: scam
    celle-là → **lacelle**: that one

Here are some frequently used verlan words:

    merci → **cimer**: thank you
    merde → **demer:** shit
    beau gosse → **gossebo**: handsome guy
    famille → **mifa**: family
    bête → **teubé:** dumb/stupid
    bizarre → **zarbi**: weird

For one-syllable words, a different technique is used. Usually, you need to pronounce the silent "e" (called a *schwa*) at the end of the word before changing it into verlan. If the word doesn't end with a schwa, you need to add one:

louche → **chelou**: strange/shady
noir → **noireu** → **renoi** : black

- **TRANSFORMATION AND SHORTENING**

Now, let's try putting all these verlan tricks together to create new words. First transform the word into verlan, then shorten it:

femme → **femmeuh** → **meufa** → **meuf**: woman, wife, or girlfriend
fête → **fêteuh** → **teufé** → **teuf**: party

- **RE-VERLANIZATION**

Sometimes words are put through the verlan process again, creating re-verlanized words. For the grand finale, here's a six-part transformation that results in the most common verlan word used in France today:

arabe → **arabeuh** → **beurahah** → **beura** → **beur**: Arab

You'll hear *beur* often enough, but sometimes the verlan process may continue:

beur → **beure** → **rebeu**: Arab

- **FOREIGN INFLUENCES**

France has a significant Romani population, often referred to as gypsies. Despite common stereotypes, these travelers have an unfair reputation as criminals, beggars, and thieves. Regardless, the French have adopted many Romani words into their language.

girl/girlfriend

xv

gadji

boy/boyfriend
gadjo

to steal
chourer
chouraver
ravchou (in verlan)

thief
chouraveur, chouraveuse

robbery
chourave

knife
chouri
surin

to denounce/to report
poucaver

traitor
poucaveur, poucaveuse

to f**k
bouillaver

That guy is so shady.
Il est trop chelou ce gadjo.

Someone stole my car!
On m'a chouré ma voiture !

Martine got mugged in the street, the guy pulled out a knife.
Martine s'est faite agressée dans la rue, le gars a sorti un surin.

- **BLACK SHEEPS**

Les *pieds-noirs*, meaning "black feet," were French colonists and settlers from North Africa who returned to France with their mixed families. The most famous pied-noir was Nobel Prize-winning author Albert Camus, known for his works *L'Etranger* and *La Peste*. Here are some words of Arabic origin that you'll often hear in French:

baggage/stuff
barda

town/village
bled

hashish
haschich
chichon

a little/tiny bit
chouia

dog
clebs
clebard

money
flouze

cock
zob

Quentin comes from a small town lost in the middle of France.
Quentin vient d'un petit bled paumé au milieu de la France.

I'm not that hungry anymore but I'll take a tiny bit of dessert.
Je n'ai plus très faim mais je prendrai un chouia de dessert.

Can that dog stop barking? I can't sleep!
Qu'il arrête d'aboyer ce clebard, j'arrive pas à dormir !

1. Greetings & Salutations!

- **HELLO!**

You probably shouldn't use French slang with strangers, especially if they're over thirty – unless you want to annoy them. When in doubt, just say *bonjour*. Once you've gotten to know someone, you can use some of these slang expressions. Side note for all you female readers: using these with strangers will definitely get you noticed!

Hi
Salut

Hey!/Yo!
Ho !

Hey, you/Hey, baby
Coucou

Yo, dudes/guys!
Oh, les gars !

Yo, girls!
Oh, les filles !

Yo dudes, how's it going?
Yo les gars, comment ça va ?

Yo girls, wanna go to a party with us?
Oh les filles, vous voulez aller à une teuf avec nous ?

- **ON THE PHONE**

Hello?
Âllo ?

Hey!
Salut !

Hello, who is it?
Âllo, c'est qui à l'appareil ?

- **FROM MORNING TO EVENING**

In French, there are many informal ways to say "good morning" and "good evening."

Mornin', honey!
Bonjour, mon chéri (to a man)
Bonjour, ma chérie (to a woman)

Hey, babe-good morning!
Bonjour, toi !

Mornin'!
Jour !

Evenin'!
'Soir !

Night!
Bonne nuit !

Evenin'! What you cookin'?
'Soir ! Tu cuisines quoi ?

Night, sweet dreams.
Bonne nuit, fais de beaux rêves.

- **KISSING HELLO**

You probably know that the French greet each other with little pecks on the cheek, like pigeons doing a mating dance. This is similar to the American "college hug" – which the French find odd, thinking you're coming on to them if you try it.

Women exchange these kisses with all friends, both male and female, when they see them for the first time each day. If you kiss one person in a group, you should kiss everyone (as long as they're about your age). Just go cheek to cheek and make a kissing sound in the air; don't actually touch your lips to their cheek.

For men, it's a bit different. They use this kiss to greet female friends and family only. Among male friends, they just shake hands.

shake hands
se serrer la main

to kiss "hello"
faire la bise

"kisses" (like on the phone or a postcard)
bisous
bises

to kiss on the mouth
embrasser sur la bouche

I think we know each other well enough, we can kiss hello.
Je pense qu'on se connaît suffisamment, on peut se faire la bise.

I kissed him hello and he tried to kiss me on the mouth!
Je lui ai fait la bise, et il a essayé de m'embrasser sur la bouche !

- **TEXT MESSAGING**

Later
A+ (à plus)

Catch you later
A12C4 (à un de ces quatre)

LOL
MDR (mort de rire)

Screw you
TG (ta gueule)

My ass
(.) (mon cul)

Kiss my ass
JTMD (je t'emmerde)

F**k you/Go f**ck yourself
VTFF (va te faire foutre)

Don't worry
Tkt (t'inquiète)

Someone
qqn (quelqu'un)

Something
qqchose/qqch (quelque chose)

I can't (anymore)

JPP (je peux pas or j'en peux plus)

- **WHAT'S UP?**

In English, when asked "what's up?" we usually give a one-word answer because, let's face it, nobody really cares. But in France, they'll assume you actually want to know how they're doing and expect you to give a real answer too. My advice: be polite and answer but avoid going into too much detail about personal issues.

How's it goin'?
Ça va ?

How you doin'?
Tu vas bien ?

Long time, no see!
Ça fait longtemps, dis donc !

Watcha up to?
Qu'est-ce que tu fais ?
Qu'est-ce que tu fabriques ?

Nothing much.
Pas grand chose.

Same shit, different day.
Comme d'hab'.

How you been?
Alors, qu'est-ce que tu deviens ?

So-so
Comme ci, comme ça

Same as always, man
Ben, toujours pareil

Good!

Ça roule !

What's the word?
Quelles sont les nouvelles ?

Same old bullshit.
Toujours le même bordel.

What the hell are you up to?
Qu'est-ce que tu fous ?

What the hell are you doing here?
Qu'est-ce que tu fous là ?

- **GOODBYE!**

Bye!
Bye ! Salut !

See ya!
Ciao !

Later!
À plus !

Catch you later!
À un de ces quatre !

See ya tomorrow!
À demain !

Call me.
On s'appelle.

Let's roll
On bouge
On y va

I'm outta here

Je me casse

It was nice to catch up, catch you later!
C'était chouette de se voir, à un de ces quatre !

The party sucks, I'm outta here.
La teuf est naze, je me casse.

- **GETTING ATTENTION**

Look!
Regarde !

Check that out!
Regarde-moi ça !

Hey, kid!
Oh, jeune !

Hey, babe!
Salut, ma beauté !

C'mere for a sec.
Viens voir une minute.

I gotta tell you something.
J'ai un truc à te dire.

Please, Sir/Madam
Monsieur/Madame, s'il vous plaît !

- **APOLOGIES**

I'm sorry.
Je suis désolé(e).

Sorry

Pardon

To forgive
Pardonner

Whoops!
Oups !

That sucks!
Ça craint !

Oh, shit!
Merde !

Whoops, sorry! I hadn't seen you!
Oups, pardon ! Je vous avais pas vu !

I'm really sorry for being late.
Je suis vraiment désolée d'être en retard.

- **KEEPING IT CLASSY**

Politeness in France is mainly for work, with strangers, or when there's an age difference. With friends, you can usually be more relaxed. However, misunderstandings can happen with different languages and cultures. So, to avoid awkward moments, it's good to have some polite phrases ready.

'Scuse me
Excusez-moi

Don't worry 'bout it
T'inquiète

Nevermind
Laisse tomber

'Scuse my shitty french
Excuse mon français merdique

Pardon my french!
Pardon, ça m'a échappé !

Chill out!
Calmos !

Please
S'il vous plaît
S'il te plaît

I owe you one.
Je te revaudrai ça.

Don't worry 'bout it, I don't blame you.
T'inquiète, je t'en veux pas.

You know what? Nevermind, let's drop it.
Tu sais quoi ? Laisse tomber.

'Scuze-me, I am lost. Can you help me?
Excusez-moi, je suis perdue. Pouvez-vous m'aider ?

2. Everyday Interactions

First things first. Before you make a mistake, let's go over what to do and not do when meeting locals. While children might give you a hug, French teens and adults won't. So, why no hugs?

When you first meet someone, people usually shake hands. After that, they switch to kissing on the cheeks, which is the typical French greeting. This happens between almost everyone except straight guys. If you're introduced to a friend of a good friend, you'll go straight to kissing based on your friend's judgment.

It's interesting that hugs are seen as too personal, while kisses are common once you've broken the ice. Although hugs involve direct contact, kisses bring you close to the mouth, making them more intimate. This practice of kissing actually began in ancient Rome to mark agreements. But beware, the number of kisses can vary: usually two on alternating cheeks, but sometimes three or four. Even the French get confused about the number of kisses, as it depends on social status, region, and age.

Also, watch out for the kissing technique. Instead of touching lips directly, place your cheek next to theirs with your lips puckered. Ladies, be aware that some French men might make a mistake on purpose to get closer to you.

- **FRIENDLY FRENCH**

In America, you might make "friends" by commenting on someone's Instagram pic with "GORGEOUS!!!" In France, people are more old-fashioned and prefer to get to know you first. However, if you do manage to make French friends, they'll be loyal and stick with you.

friend
amie(e)

best friend
meilleur(e) ami(e)

a buddy/pal
un(e) pote
un(e) copain, copine

boyfriend
mec
copain

girlfriend
meuf
copine

We've been buddies since kindergarten.
On est potes depuis la maternelle.

My boyfriend is coming to pick me up.
Mon mec vient me chercher.

Nathan has a new girlfriend.
Nathan a une nouvelle meuf.

• COOL & FUNNY STUFF

You can use these expressions for things you like or find funny. Just remember that the French generally don't laugh in public as much or as loudly as Americans do.

It is…
C'est…

> **nice**
> *sympa*
>
> **cool**
> *cool*
>
> **great**
> *génial*
> *super*
>
> **perfect**
> *impec'*
>
> **funny**
> *rigolo*

Camille's report was perfect.
Le rapport de Camille était impec'.

Your new apartment is so cool, I love it!
Trop cool ton nouvel appart, je kiffe trop !

• THE FRENCH TYPES

He/she is…
Il/elle est…

> **a stand-up guy**
> *un mec droit/correct*

a sweet girl
une nana gentille

a moron
un abruti

a kick-ass
un(e) fayot(e)

a butt-licker
un lèche-cul

a show-off
un(e) frimeur, frimeuse

This employee is such a moron!
Quel abruti cet employé !

Marion's boyfriend is a real show-off.
Le copain de Marion est grave frimeur.

• FORMALITIES

Sir
Monsieur

Ma'am
Madame

Miss, Ms.
Mademoiselle

There is no French equivalent for "Ms." – just *Mademoiselle* and *Madame*. As a general rule of thumb, use *Mademoiselle* for women who look under thirty to avoid any issues.

Dr.
Docteur
In France, only medical doctors use Dr. with their names.

doc
toubib

Mr. President
Monsieur le président

cop
flic
keuf

boss
patron
chef

Good morning sir, how are you?
Bonjour Monsieur, comment allez-vous ?

My boss is the big dude who's in a bad mood.
Mon patron c'est le grand bonhomme qui tire la tête.

• FAMILY

The concept of family is very important in France, especially in the South. People are close to their entire family, including extended relatives. Kids often stay with their parents into adulthood until they marry or move in with their partners.

dad/daddy
papa

mom/mommy
maman

stepdad/stepmom
beau-père, belle-mère

'rents
vieux

bro
frérot
frangin

sis
frangine

teen
ado

grandpa
pépé
papi

kid
gamin
gosse
morveux, morveuse

There are many slang words for kids. While *gamin*, *gosse*, and *poupon* refer to good children, *morveux*, *mouflet*, *marmot*, *moutard*, and *moustique* describe bad kids, hinting at the mess and noise they make.

Mom, can I go out tonight?
Maman, est-ce que je peux sortir ce soir ?

My grandpa is turning 100 this year!
Mon papi va avoir 100 ans cette année !

These kids are getting on my nerves! All they do is cry!
Ils me gavent ces moutards ! Ils ne font que pleurer !

- **THE FRENCH POPULATION**

The following words are offensive, derogatory, and racist. While you might hear them, especially in the South or countryside, you should never use them. They are listed here for awareness purposes only.

Blacks

les blacks
les noirs
les renois (verlan of noirs)

Asians
les jaunes
les bridés
les bouffeurs de riz

Red skins
les peaux rouges

Italians
les rital
les macaroni

Portuguese
les porto

Germans
les oches
les fritz

British
les roast-beef

Americans
les ricain(e)s
les amerloques

Arabs
les beurs

Jews
les youpins

Chinese
les chinetoques
les niakoués

Japanese

les japs

Americans always attract attention wherever they go, they are not liked by the French.
Les ricains se font remarquer partout où ils vont, ils ne sont pas aimés de français.

We're in the Italian neighborhood.
On est dans le quartier des rital.

Paris is getting invaded by the Chinese!
Paris est envahi de chinetoques !

- **MAKING CONVERSATION**

to go
faire

to understand/to 'get' something
piger
capter

to tell
chanter

to ramble
radoter

to seem right
coller

to hit a snag
coincer

to not be quite right
ne pas tourner rond

problem
blème (abbr. of problème)

to tell
accoucher

to spit out
cracher

I went home and my dad went "what's that tattoo?!"
Je suis rentrée et mon père m'a fait "c'est quoi ce tatouage ?!"

You really don't get anything I'm saying.
Tu piges vraiment rien à ce que je dis.

Something doesn't seem right in his story.
Y a quelque chose qui tourne pas rond dans son histoire.

3. Food Fixation

Ask anyone where the best food in the world comes from and they'll probably say France. Good cooking may be in their blood, but keeping this reputation takes hard work. The finest food often involves harsh treatment of the ingredients. For example, making *foie gras* is now considered abuse and is illegal in many parts of the US and UK. However, except for a few PETA supporters, most French people would laugh if you called *foie gras* cruel. Other French favorites include *les cuisses de grenouille* (frog's legs) and *les escargots à l'ail* (snails in garlic butter). As the French say, *il faut goûter de tout* ("one must taste everything" or "don't knock it 'til you've tried it"). *La tête de veau vinaigrette* (calf's head in vinegar dressing) was a favorite dish of former President Jacques Chirac. And you thought Clinton's love for McDonald's was strange!

restaurant
table
resto

to die of hunger
crever de faim

to be hungry/starving
avoir la dalle

to grab a bite
manger un morceau

to snack on something
grignoter qqchose

snack
casse-croûte

feast
gueuleton

to eat
bouffer

all you can eat
à gogo

cook
cuistot

junk food
malbouffe

fast food
fast food

Food is still a big part of French culture, but fast food is becoming increasingly common. The French are also losing their two-hour lunch break, which leaves them less time to cook. As a result, families spend less time together, and obesity is on the rise. However, the "French paradox" – which entails eating cheese, creamy sauces, and drinking lots of red wine all the while staying perfectly slim – still holds true in most places.

to stuff oneself

se goinfrer
se bâfrer

fish
poiscaille

Yum! That was…
Miam ! C'était...

    a good meal
    un bon repas

    really tasty
    vraiment bon

    delicious
    délicieux

    scrumptious
    un régal

    filling
    bien assez

Yum-yum!
Miam miam !

It's really good!
C'est super bon !

Yuck!
Beurk !

It's disgusting.
C'est dégueulasse.

I'm too lazy to cook, why don't we go to a restaurant tonight?
J'ai la flemme de cuisiner, on va au resto ce soir ?

I haven't eaten since 6 am this morning, I am starving!
J'ai pas mangé depuis 6h ce matin, j'ai trop la dalle !

I could eat two big pizzas.
Je pourrais bouffer deux grosses pizzas.

Myriam went to buy biscuits to snack on the road.
Myriam est allée acheter des biscuits pour grignoter sur la route.

- ## AT THE RESTAURANT

Bring me...
Apportez-moi...

> **the menu**
> *la carte*

> **the check**
> *l'addition*

Can I speak to...
Puis-je parler au...

> **the manager**
> *patron*
> *manager*

> **the chef**
> *chef*

> **the cook**
> *cuistot*

> **the waiter/the waitress**
> *serveur, serveuse*

> **the wine steward**
> *sommelier*

Can we order?
On peut commander?

What do you recommend?
Qu'est-ce que vous recommandez?

• HOW DO YOU LIKE YOUR MEAT?

In France, meat is either served very rare or well done, with little in between. They don't even have words for medium or medium-rare. Most French people prefer their meat rare (much rarer than Americans), partly because French meat is very tender.

very rare
bleu

rare
saignant

medium well
à point

well-done
bien cuit

• FRENCH CLASSICS

Just as a hamburger with fries is the ultimate American dish, *steak frites* (steak with fries) is the go-to meal in France. However, the French consider fries to be Belgian and it's common to hear Belgians being called *mangeurs de frites* (fry eaters). Besides this national dish, France has many regional specialties:

The Northwest

Can I get some...?
Je peux avoir...?

Les Moules Frites
A big bowl of steaming, fragrant mussels accompanied by crunchy fries.

Les Coquilles Saint-Jacques
Scallops cooked in butter with onions and shallots, topped with grated cheese.

La Tarte Tatin
The French version of apple pie, served upside down and caramelized.

Les Crêpes
You can have them for lunch, topped with cheese, ham, and eggs, or as dessert, covered in chocolate, Nutella, sugar, or jam.

The East

You gotta try the...
Tu devrais essayer...

La Choucroute
Originating in the Alsace-Lorraine region, this dish is served as a big plate of sauerkraut with saucisses de Francfort, a slice of jambon, and steamed potatoes.

La Quiche Lorraine
Basically a ham and cheese quiche.

Le Bœuf Bourguignon
A classic French stew of cubed beef slow-cooked in red wine and broth.

Les Escargots de Bourgogne
A French delicacy: snails cooked in lots of butter and parsley.

Provence & Riviera

The local specialties are...
Les spécialités locales sont...

La Salade Niçoise
A classic salad served with fresh vegetables, boiled egg, tuna, anchovies, and olive oil.

La Bouillabaisse
The French version of Gumbo, with fish, potatoes, and soup.

La Daube Provençale
Red wine-marinated beef, cut in strips and served with pasta or rice.

Southwest

You've never tried...?
Tu n'as jamais goûté...?

Roquefort
A strong blue cheese.

Cassoulet
A nourishing winter dish made with duck, sausage, goose fat, and beans; sop up the drippings with crusty bread.

The Alps

Let's feast on...
Gavons-nous de...

Fondue Savoyarde
A traditional French dish from the Savoy region, made by melting a mix of cheeses (typically Gruyère, Emmental, and Comté) with white wine and garlic. Great after skiing!

Gratin Dauphinois
Gratin-style potatoes with sour cream and oven-melted cheese.

- **CHEESE**

France has a larger variety of cheese than any other country. Like wine, every region has its own variety. They come in all shapes, colors, and smells, from mild to those that smell worse than sweaty animals in a barnyard. Cheese is so important to French culture that they use it in sayings, like *N'en fais pas tout un fromage*, which means "don't make a big deal out of it."

Pass the...

Passe-moi...

Cut me a slice of...
Coupe-moi un morceau de...

Brie
A mild, creamy and popular cow's milk cheese.

Camembert
Also from cow's milk and relatively mild.

Gruyère
Basically a Swiss cheese made from goat's milk. It's dense and sharp, and comes in small servings.

Bleu d'Auvergne
Originating from the central Auvergne region, a smoother type of blue cheese.

Saint-Nectaire
Another classic Auvergnat and the most commonly produced farmer cheese in France.

Mimolette
Made in the North of France near the Belgian border, this cow's milk cheese features a taste and orange color that makes it similar to our cheddars.

Boursin
Famous soft cheese from Normandy, with a pepper touch.

- **COFFEE**

an espresso
un express

a double espresso
un double

an expresso with a drop of cream
une noisette

a coffee diluted with extra water
un allongé
un café américain

an American coffee with milk
un café au lait

I'll have a coffee diluted with extra water to go please.
Je prendrai un allongé à emporter, s'il vous plaît.

- **SANDWICHES**

Except for the *Bagnat* and the *Club*, which are made with hamburger buns and sliced bread, all French sandwiches use baguettes. While there are places called *sandwicheries* that serve – you guessed it – sandwiches, you can get a sandwich almost anywhere that sells food.

I'm craving a…
J'ai trop envie de…

Croque-Monsieur
The most famous French sandwich. It's basically just a grilled ham and cheese sandwich, but you have to eat it with a fork because it comes smothered in melted Gruyère cheese.

Croque-Madame
Same as above, but with a fried egg on top.

Pain Bagnat
A delicious concoction of anchovies, tomatoes, black olives, olive oil, and onions served on a hamburger bun.

Parisien
Ham and butter: the original version of Parisian "fast food."

4. All About Culture

- **MOVIES**

France may only have the sixth-largest film industry in the world, but we actually owe movies to France, as French brothers Auguste and Louis Lumière invented the film camera. French movie genres are similar to English ones: *un film d'action* (action film), *un film d'horreur* (horror film), *un film romantique* (romantic film), *un film de science fiction* (sci-fi film), and so on. If you dislike *les comédies musicales* (musicals), you can jokingly tell your friends that this book says they don't exist in France.

ticket
billet

big screen
grand écran

the line
la queue

Wanna watch a movie?
On se mate un film ?

Wanna go see a flick?
On va au cinoche ?

How 'bout a.....?
Ça te dirait...?

> **cartoon**
> *un dessin animé*
>
> **tearjerker**
> *un film à l'eau de rose*
>
> **grandma movie**
> *un film cucul la praline*
>
> **chick flick**
> *un film pour les gonzesses*
>
> **dubbed movie**
> *un film doublé*
> *un film en v.f. (en version française)*
> Except in Paris, foreign films in theaters and on TV are usually dubbed.
>
> **movie with subtitles**
> *un film en v.o. (en version originale)*
>
> **skin flick/ porn**
> *un film de cul*

- **FRENCHIFIED AMERICAN CLASSICS**

In France, American films sometimes keep their original English titles and sometimes get totally new – and weird – ones. Here a some examples:

Meet the Parents
Mon beau-père et moi

There's Something About Mary
Mary à tout Prix

Jaws
Les Dents de la mer

Good Fellas
Les Affranchis

Shawshank Redemption
Les Évadés

Die Hard
Piège de Cristal

The Bourne Ultimatum
La Vengeance dans la peau

Groundhog Day
Un jour sans fin

The Departed
Les Infiltrés

Jaws is currently being screened in cinemas.
Y a Les Dents de la mer qui est actuellement au ciné.

What's the original title of The Revenge in the Skin?
C'est quoi le titre original de La Vengeance dans la peau ?

- **COMICS**

Graphic novels are seen as an art form in France and have a long history there. In French bookstores, you'll find a comics section where both adults and kids enjoy reading for hours. Classic French comic heroes include the clumsy *Gaston*

Lagaffe, the adventurer *Corto Maltese*, and the fast-drawing cowboy *Lucky Luke*, who "shoots faster than his shadow."

Do you have any…?
Avez-vous…?

comic books
des bandes dessinées

comics
des BD

new editions
des nouvelles éditions

first editions
premières éditions

Who's your favorite…?
Qui est ton…favori/préféré ?

superhero
super héros

villain
méchant

sidekick
frère d'armes

mutant
mutant

monster
monstre

Do you have the first editions of the Tintin Comics?
Vous avez les premières éditions des BD Tintin ?

Martin is looking for the new Astérix and Obélix comics.
Martin cherche les nouvelles BD Astérix et Obélix.

- **MUSIC**

Did you know that France is the second-largest market for rap in the world, after the US? Or that the Stade de France soccer stadium near Paris is one of Europe's biggest concert venues? Or that most French people don't give a f**k about country music? Now you do!

I'm totally into…
Je kiffe grave le…

I can't stand that…
Je peux pas supporter ce/cette…

I'm in love with that…
J'adore ce/cette…

> **musician**
> *musicien(ne)*
>
> **lead singer**
> *chanteur/chanteuse*
>
> **drummer**
> *batteur*
>
> **bassist**
> *bassiste*
>
> **guitar player**
> *guitariste*
>
> **song**
> *chanson*
>
> **cover song**
> *reprise*
>
> **lyrics**
> *paroles*

tunes
'zique

I love Pink Floyd!
Je kiffe trop Pink Floyd !

What's the name of the band making these tunes?
Comment s'appelle le groupe qui fait cette 'zique ?

• GOOD OLD-FASHIONED GAMES

board games
jeux de société

chess
échecs

card games
jeux de carte

pool
billard

darts
fléchettes

pinball
flipper

foosball
baby foot

Should we do a board game night?
On se fait une soirée jeux de société ?

Max holds the pinball record.
Max tient le record du flipper.

- **GAMERS & TECHIES**

Some things can't help but be universal. French teens are big into gaming now. It's hard to find an Internet café not filled with teenagers in headsets, shouting about their latest gaming achievements without moving their eyes from the screen and their hands from the joystick.

I'll kick your ass at...
Je vais te défoncer aux/à

    video games
    jeux vidéo

    Playstation
    la Playstation

Don't touch my...
Touche pas à mon...

    laptop
    ordi portable

    cell phone
    portable

    iPod
    iPod ("EEE-pod")

    hard drive
    disque dur

wi-fi
wifi ("weee-feee")

text message
texto

I'm in a rush, I need to send a text to my boyfriend.
Je suis à la bourre, faut que j'envoie un texto à mon copain.

- **TELEVISION**

You can't avoid trashy American TV just by going to France. Most popular American shows, and even some that got low ratings in the US, are shown there dubbed in French – obviously.

Let's watch…
On se mate…

… is my favorite show
… est mon show préféré

> **American Idol**
> *La Star Academy*
>
> **Survivor**
> *Koh Lanta*
>
> **Wheel of Fortune**
> *La Roue de la Fortune*
>
> **The Price Is Right**
> *Le Juste Prix*

Hurry up, I don't want to miss Survivor!
Magne-toi, je ne veux pas rater Koh Lanta !

- **SPORTS**

In France, soccer is called *football* or just *foot*, and it's by far the most popular sport. Nothing else even comes close. Other popular sports include tennis, rugby, cycling, judo, skiing, and Formula One racing.

I play…
Je joue au…

Do you play…?
Est-ce que tu joues au..?

Wanna go play some...?
Tu veux jouer au...?

Let's watch the... match
Regardons le match de...

> **soccer**
> *football*
> *foot*
>
> **basketball**
> *basket*
>
> **volleyball**
> *volley*
>
> **bowling**
> *bowling ("boo-ling")*
>
> **football**
> *football américain*
>
> **hockey**
> *hockey sur glace*

Should we go bowling this weekend?
On se fait une partie de bowling ce week-end ?

Soccer is not the same thing as football.
Le foot c'est pas la même chose que le football américain.

- **LIVE FROM THE STADIUM**

If you get a chance to see a soccer game in France, take it. The French national team plays at the Stade de France, just North of Paris. The two most famous pro teams are Paris-Saint Germain (PSG), which plays at the Parc des Princes in Southwest Paris, and the Olympique de Marseille (OM), which plays at the Stade Vélodrome on the Mediterranean coast. The rivalry between PSG and OM is as intense as the Yankees vs. the Red Sox – except

Red Sox fans don't usually clash with Yankees fans with bats and bricks at rest stops.

the players
les joueurs

the teams
les équipes

Let's go to...
Allons à...

> **a game**
> *un match*
>
> **a match**
> *une partie*
>
> **the championship game/the final**
> *la finale*
>
> **the tournament**
> *au tournoi*
>
> **the stadium**
> *au stade*

He's leaving at the match's halftime.
Il part à la mi-temps du match.

This match is so boring.
On se fait chier pendant ce match.

- **THE FANS**

The French believe in unions so fan clubs are organized in the stands, equipped with microphones, singing chants by heart. They support their team by cheering and booing the opposing team (they whistle instead of booing). They can even influence team decisions or push for more investment in new players.

37

the stands
les tribunes

the fans
les supporteurs
les fans

to bet
parier

the referee
l'arbitre

fan clubs
les clubs de supporters
fan clubs

goal
but

to score
marquer

Who's playing?
Qui joue ?

Who scored the goal?
Qui a marqué le but ?

That goal was insane!
Ce but était ouf !

5. The Wrong Side of the Law

You're unlikely to get into serious trouble with the law in France, but if you do, don't expect an *Inspector Clouseau* or *Hercule Poirot* to help you out. French police have a reputation not much better than the LAPD's. You definitely don't want to call your Grandma at midnight to tell her you're in a French prison and need bail. It's better to stay out of trouble altogether, as spending twenty-four hours in a French cell isn't pleasant.

Drugs are less of a problem in France compared to the US, but you'll still see some addicts on the streets at night. Marijuana is very common, and it's likely the only drug you'll encounter there. However, cigarettes and alcohol are also widely used. French drunks can be quite a sight, often stumbling around with their pants undone and urinating in public – which is considered a normal behavior there. While public indecency is frowned upon in the US, it's common in France for men to urinate almost anywhere.

- **TOBACCO**

ciggy
clope

smoke
sèche

Do you have a lighter to light my ciggy?
T'as un briquet pour allumer ma clope ?

- **MARY-JANE**

Paris isn't like Amsterdam when it comes to drugs. The French government takes drug laws seriously, and people are careful on the streets. Still, many French people smoke weed and hash. Most of it comes from Morocco, and the quality can vary.

a joint
un joint
un oinj (in verlan)
un bedo

a doobie
un pétard
un beuze

a spliff
un spliff

weed/pot
herbe
beuh (in verlan)

hash
le hasch
le haschisch
du shit

to be high
planer

weed
la fumette

to grow marijuana
faire pousser de la marie-jeanne

Do you know a dealer?
Tu connais un dealer ?

I'm getting a little stoned.
Je commence à être un peu défoncé(e).

I was so high, I ate a whole pack of cookies.
Je planais tellement que j'ai bouffé un paquet de cookies entier.

- **THE HARDCORE STUFF**

While smoking weed is somewhat accepted in France, cocaine or Ecstasy will definitely land you in jail.

coke
la coke
coca

crack
le crack

white powder
la poudre blanche

a line
une ligne

a rail
un rail

heroin
l'héroine

to shoot up
se shooter

pills
des pilules

drug addict
toxico

ecstasy/x
l'ecsta'

I was told you have coke.
On m'a dit que tu avais de la coke.

Man, you're an addict.
Mon vieux, t'es accro'.

Nadia's new boyfriend is a drug addict.
Le nouveau copain de Nadia est un toxico.

- **THE PLAYERS**

cop/pig
flic
flicaille
poulet

corrupt cop
ripou (verlan for pourri)

spy/mole
taupe

gang chief
caid

to catch
choper

on the run
en cavale

to be caught red-handed
pris la main dans le sac

to arrest / to pinch
pincer

to be in custody
être en GAV (garde à vue)

bribe
pot-de-vin
dessous de table

to fix
magouiller

schemer
magouilleur, magouilleuse

to be duped
se faire embobiner

someone who got ripped off
pigeon

Pigeons aren't just found in Piazza San Marco in Venice. French monuments also attract these birds, alongside hordes of tourists who flock to souvenir shops. Tourists crowd monuments, parks, and public places, especially in August, much like pigeons drawn to breadcrumbs. Because of this, the word *pigeon* is now used to describe anyone who gets tricked in a deal.

to rip someone off
plumer qqn

Let's get out of here, the cops are coming!

Tirons-nous, y a les flics qui arrivent !

Careful they don't catch you.
Fais gaffe de pas te faire choper.

Kevin's uncle got pinched because he was dealing drugs.
L'oncle de Kevin s'est fait pincer car il dealait de la drogue.

- **WEAPONS & CRIMINALS**

Even though crime rates are going up, the French don't feel the need to keep guns at home for safety. You won't find bullets in corner stores, and if you do, buying and owning a gun will require more than just a driver's license. While tourists might face risks like armed muggings, France is generally safe. Unlike in the US, where gun violence is a major issue, France's strict gun laws make it safer. So leave your gun at home – France is not a dangerous place, and the worst you might encounter is getting mugged in the *métro*.

piece (gun)
flingue

to gun down
flinguer

to commit suicide
se flinguer

to kill
butter

to destroy
bousiller

jail
placard
carpla (in verlan)
taule

to escape

se faire la belle/la malle

My boss is going to kill me.
Mon patron va me butter.

I was walking in a street in New York and a guy took out his piece and assaulted a woman.
Je marchais dans une rue à New York et un gars a sorti son flingue et a agressé une femme.

Drop it, he's a head taller than you, he'll kill you!
Laisse tomber, il fait une tête de plus que toi, il va te butter !

Jacques's cousin robbed a house and got caught; he's in jail.
Le cousin de Jacques a cambriolé une maison et s'est fait chopé ; il est en taule.

6. The French Look

- **THE SEXY FRENCH**

The French ideal isn't too different from other countries. While the typical American man is tall, dark, and handsome, the ideal Frenchman is blond and blue-eyed. For women, the French taste is pretty standard: a nice figure with a small waist.

He/She is...
Il/Elle est...

> **handsome (guys)**
> *beau*
>
> **beautiful (girls)**
> *belle*

cute
mignon(ne)

really cute (girls)
craquante

totally hot (girls)
bandante

gorgeous
canon

a hottie
une bombe

pretty
jolie

sexy
sexy

stylish
à la mode

really fashionable
glamour

hip
branché(e)

He/She has...
Il/Elle a...

a lean face
un visage fin

a friendly or likable face
une bonne piffe

a good "mug"
une bonne gueule

a square jaw (guys)
un visage carré

a hot figure
une très belle silhouette

good measurements
de bonnes mensurations

Did you see the handsome dude that just walked in?
T'as vu le beau gosse qui vient d'entrer ?

Myriam is cute, I will ask for her number.
Myriam est mignonne, je vais lui demander son num.

Wow, you look gorgeous!
Waouw, t'es trop canon !

- **BODY TYPES**

He/She is...
Il/Elle est...

   tall
   grand(e)

   well-built (girls)
   bien foutue

   buff (guys)
   baraqué

   little
   petit(e)

   short
   court(e)

   frail (guys)/delicate (girls)

délicat(e)

scrawny
un sac d'os

hunchback
bossu(e)

tanned
bronzé(e)

pale
pâle

long-haired
chevelu(e)

hairy
poilu(e)

chunky/chubby
enveloppé(e)

fat
gros, grosse

skinny
maigre

lean/slim
mince

anorexic
anorexique
squelettique

I'm the hairiest in our family.
Je suis le plus poilu dans ma famille.

Jean has become really buff since he started going to the gym.
Jean est devenu super baraqué depuis qu'il va à la salle de sport.

Carl just came back from a month in France, he got chubby!
Carl vient de rentrer d'un mois en France, il est bien enveloppé !

- **THE NASTY FRENCH**

If you think French people are always stylish and slim like in TV commercials or films, you might be surprised. France has its fair share of people who don't fit that glamorous image.

He/She has...
Il/Elle a...

> **beady eyes**
> *de petits yeux*
>
> **a fugly "grill"**
> *une tronche pas possible*
>
> **a stubby body and short legs**
> *un corps trapu et de petites jambes*
>
> **a nasty mop of hair**
> *une sale tignasse*
>
> **a bad figure**
> *un physique désagréable*
> *mal foutu(e)*
>
> **a tiny head**
> *une petite tête*
>
> **a big head**
> *une grosse tête*

He/She is...
Il/Elle est...

> **ugly**
> *moche*

cheum (verlan of moche)

hideous
laid(e)

homely
un/une laideron(ne)
un/une mocheté(e)

dirty
sale

filthy
crade

a dog
un thon

repulsive (guys)
répugnant

completely gross (guys)
ignoble

nasty (guys)
immonde

My history professor really has a nasty mop of hair.
Mon professeur d'Histoire a vraiment une sale tignasse.

Why are you flirting with her? She has a bad figure!
Pourquoi tu la dragues ? Elle est mal foutue !

That chick is ugly, she's really a dog.
Cette meuf est grave moche, c'est vraiment un thon.

- **SERVING LOOKS**

If you think all French people are super stylish, ready to hit the runway of a fashion show, you might be disappointed. While Paris is known as the fashion capital of the world and French designers set global trends, most people don't wear high fashion every day.

In reality, the French do care about their appearance, but you won't see everyone in haute couture. Most French women age gracefully and look stylish at any age, and French men, especially Parisians, also take pride in their appearance. Whether you wear jeans and a designer T-shirt or are dressed in reggae gear, keeping a unique style is important. Nowadays, most people shop in department stores rather than high-end boutiques and spend on brand names – or at least good imitations.

to be dressed to the nines
se mettre sur son 31

outfit
tenue

suit
costard.

brand new
flambant neuf

to be trendy
être tendance

out of fashion
ringard(e)

walk
dégaine

clothes
fringues

bra
soutif

shoes
pompes
godasses

well dressed
bien sapé(e)

badly dressed
mal sapé(e)

How do you like my dress? It's brand new!
Comment tu trouves ma robe ? Elle est flambant neuve !

We're going to a fancy restaurant tonight, don't forget to be dressed to the nines!
On va à un resto chic ce soir, n'oubliez pas de vous mettre sur votre 31 !

What is he wearing? He's so badly dressed!
Qu'est-ce qu'il porte ? Il est trop mal sapé !

- **ANATOMY**

face
bouille

nose
pif

leg(s)
guibolle(s)

abs
abdos

stomach/belly
bide

tits
nichons

love handles
poignées d'amour

Your boyfriend's got a nice face.
Il a une bonne bouille ton copain.

My music professor has an enormous nose!
Mon professeur de musique a un énorme pif !

I started bodybuilding to have more abs.
Je me suis mis à la muscu pour avoir plus d'abdos.

My dad's got a big beer belly.
Mon père a un gros bide à bière.

7. Style Over Substance?

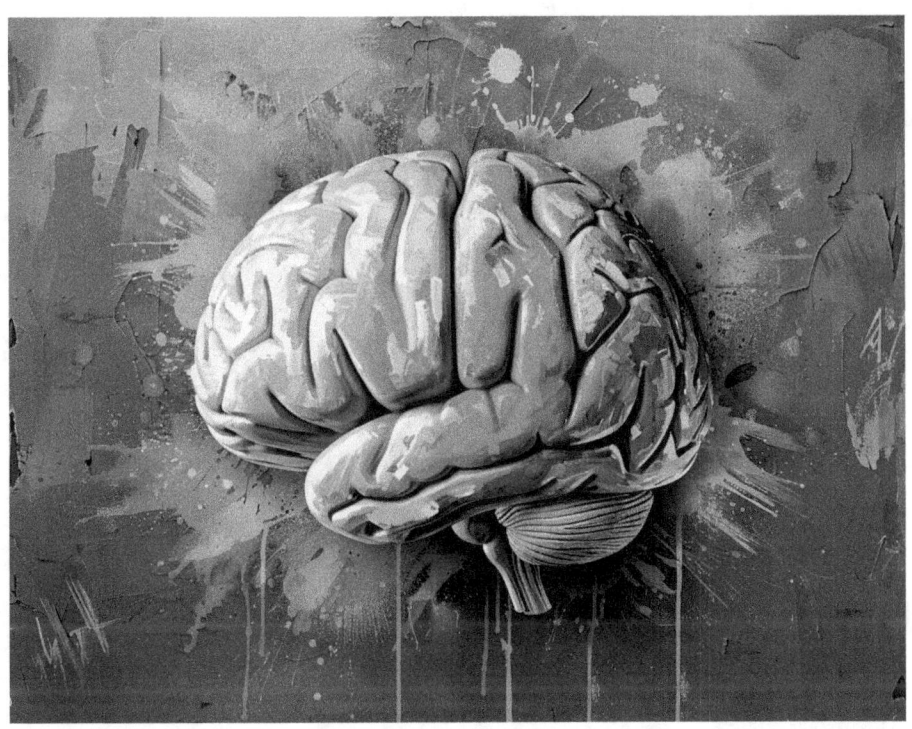

In France, even though beauty is appreciated, looks aren't everything. A person's style and how they present themselves are more important than just being attractive.

Does this mean the French care less about appearances than Americans? Not really. French people spend a lot on clothes, shoes, and beauty products. Even those living in tough neighborhoods will save or steal to get new Nikes or a Louis Vuitton bag. French women spend more on face creams and slimming products than any other women. Just check out makeup brands like L'Oréal, Clinique, and Lancôme – they're all French!

- **QUALITIES AND CHARACTER**

to have a stick up one's ass
avoir un balai dans le cul

to have a heart of stone
avoir un cœur de pierre

to not give a shit about someone
snober qqn

The word *snob* comes from the Latin term *sine nobilitas*, meaning "without nobility." Originally, it was used to distinguish wealthy people who acted like nobles but who weren't actually from noble families. Today, *snob* and *snobinard* are used to describe rich people who act superior, whether or not they have noble backgrounds.

spy
mouchard

wimp
poltron

to let people walk all over you
se faire marcher dessus

to keep quiet
se tenir à carreau

to be mad at someone
faire la gueule à qqn

to whine
pleurnicher

to be careful
faire gaffe

to get bored
s'emmerder

to be down
ne pas avoir le moral

scaredy cat
poule mouillée

ass-licker
lèche-botte/cul

to be made a fool of
être le dindon de la farce

to fool around
déconner

scum
racaille

partier
fêtard

nice guy
chic type

show-off
rouleur de mécaniques

to get on someone's nerves
mettre qqn hors de soi

to have some balls
avoir une sacrée paire de couilles

strong
balaise

to treat someone like shit
traiter qqn comme de la merde

to be lucky
avoir du bol/cul/pot

Are you done fooling around?
T'as fini de déconner ?!

He knows each professor's favorite dessert, what an ass-licker!
Il connaît les desserts préférés de chacun des professeurs, quel lèche-cul !

What happened? Why is she whining?
Qu'est-ce qu'il s'est passé ? Pourquoi elle pleurniche ?

Can we go do something ? I'm bored.
On peut aller faire quelque chose ? Je m'emmerde.

Why is Anne with Charles? Can't she see that he treats her like shit?
Pourquoi Anne est avec Charles ? Elle voit pas qu'il la traite comme de la merde ?

- **CAPABILITIES**

In French, words related to the brain, light, and technology are used to describe intelligence, while words related to female genitalia, empty objects, and vegetables tend to be used to describe stupidity.

to be able to
arriver

to manage
se démerder
se débrouiller

to be a king
être un as

genius
lumière

mastermind/ ringleader
cerveau

I don't know what to do but I'll manage.
Je sais pas quoi faire mais je vais me démerder.

This guy, he's not a genius.
Ce gars, c'est pas une lumière.

- **FEELING STUPID**

stupid
cruche

dummy
patate

to have shit for brains
avoir de la sciure à la place du cerveau

cretin
crétin(e)

to be incompetent
être largué(e)

to be lost
être paumé(e)

I am so stupid, I lost my credit card!
Quelle cruche, j'ai perdu ma carte bleue !

Michel seems completely lost, I don't think he understands anything.
Michel a l'air complètement paumé, je pense qu'il comprend rien.

- **LOSING IT**

to go gaga
perdre la boule

to be crazy
être marteau

lunatic/insane
cinglé(e)

nuts/crazy

dingue
dingo

Bells are hollow, similar to how people might think a stupid or crazy person's head is. In France, when church bells ring, they make a ding-dong sound, hence the word *dingue*.

crazy
barjot
barje

nuts
timbré(e)
givré(e)

to be out of it
être à côté de la plaque

to be crazy/out of one's mind
taré(e)

to go berserk
péter un câble/un plomb

Caroline's grandfather is going gaga.
Le grand-père de Caroline est en train de perdre la boule.

You're completely out of your mind!
Mais t'es complètement taré toi !

If he doesn't stop his noise, I will go berserk!
S'il arrête pas son boucan, je vais péter un câble !

8. The Daily French Life

France isn't a country known for bowling, but strikes are very common. Going on strike is a right that nearly everyone exercises at some point, whether they're train conductors or high school students. This practice is a big part of French culture, similar to Italy.

Strong unions, especially in industries like heavy manufacturing and state-run sectors, strike regularly. A small strike can quickly turn into a nationwide protest, or as the French call it *une grève générale*, where all workers join in. Interestingly, even though strikes often inconvenience customers, they usually get sympathy from the public. So, if you're not French and you're not used to this kind of class struggle, get ready to be frustrated because strikes always take place during the busiest travel times.

- **TIME**

to go easy
y aller mollo

to hurry
se grouiller
se magner

to be (running) late
être à la bourre

to be in a hurry
être pressé(e)

right now
illico presto

hour
plombe

one of these days
un de ces quatre

Hurry up, we're gonna be late!
Grouille-toi, on va être en retard !

Sorry I'm in a hurry, I'll call you back later.
Pardon, je suis pressée, je te rappelle plus tard.

Get down, right now! I've been waiting for ten hours!
Tu descends, illico presto ! Ça fait dix plombes que j'attends !

- **THINGS**

Le truc, le bidule, le machin, and *la chose* are life-saving words. If you can't remember a word, just use these general terms. When a word is on the tip of your tongue, *le truc* can help you keep the conversation going.

stuff/thing
truc
bidule
machin-chose

phone call
coup de fil

book
bouquin

paper/document
papelard

fake
toc

What's the name of the thing that makes pasta?
C'est quoi le nom du truc qui fait des pâtes ?

Can you lower the volume? I need to give someone a call.
Tu peux baisser le son ? Faut que je passe un coup de fil.

It's not gold; your necklace is fake.
C'est pas de l'or ; ton collier, c'est du toc.

- **CARS**

In a country that values independence, the most important object is one that gives you freedom. Just like Germans had their Volkswagen, the French had their Citroën. The French equivalent of the VW Beetle was the *deux chevaux* (two horsepower), often called *la deuch*. French authorities even nationalized major car factories like Peugeot and Citroën. Since this car was so popular, it developed many slang terms.

car
caisse
bagnole

chick magnet
aimant à femmes

slow car
bétaillère

traffic jam
bouchon

to run a stop sign/red light
brûler un stop/feu rouge

Julien bought himself a new car. It's so beautiful!
Julien s'est acheté une nouvelle caisse. Elle est trop belle !

I'm stuck in shitty traffic jam!
Je suis coincée dans les bouchons de merde !

- **TOILETS**

Where is/are..?
Où est/sont...?

the restrooms
les toilettes
les wc
les chiottes
le petit coin

the toilet paper
le papier cul/PQ

the bathroom attendant
madame pipi

the turkish toilets (squat-and-shit toilets)
les toilettes/chiottes à la turque

the public toilet
les toilettes/chiottes publiques

In big cities like Paris and Marseille, you'll see modern public toilets (shiny, tall cylinders) on the sidewalks. You insert coins to open the door and walk in. Don't try to sneak in after someone else to try to use it for free! Once the door closes, it locks and automatically cleans itself with water and disinfectant. So, unless you have a hobby of being disinfected and fumigated, I don't recommend it!

The toilets are disgusting.
Les chiottes sont dégueulasses.

We're out of toilet paper!
Il n'y a plus de PQ!

- **WORKPLACE & WORK (OR NOT)**

high school
bahut

work
taf
boulot

to work under the table
travailler au noir

to fire someone
virer qqn

to work
bosser

to do nothing
glander
ne rien foutre

to have it easy
se la couler douce

slacker
fainéant(e)

Joachim works as a supervisor in a high school.
Joachim travaille en tant que surveillant au bahut.

I can't come tonight, I have to work.
Je peux pas venir ce soir, j'ai du taf.

Karine doesn't do anything, what a slacker!
Karine ne fout rien, quelle fainéante !

- **PROFESSIONS & SOCIAL STATUS**

aristocrat
aristo

homeless person
clochard(e)
SDF (Sans Domicile Fixe)

proletarian
prolo

teacher
instit

professor
prof

middle class citizen
bourge

maid
bonniche
conchita

slave
larbin

The city is putting in place some anti-homeless furniture.
La ville est en train de mettre en place du mobilier anti-SDF (Sans Domicile Fixe).

My name is Anaïs and I'm a teacher in a Parisian high school.
Je m'appelle Anaïs et je suis instit dans un lycée parisien.

Do it yourself, I'm not your slave!
Fais-le toi-même, je suis pas ton larbin !

9. Matters of Life & Death

No one expects to fall ill while traveling in France, but if you do, you're in good hands. France has a top-notch healthcare system known as *la Sécurité Sociale*, or *la Sécu*, which covers the medical costs for everyone living in the country. If you don't qualify for la Sécu, you're covered for free by CMU, or the *Couverture Maladie Universelle*. This means everyone, no matter their job, status or income, has health insurance.

Unlike Britain's National Health Service, France doesn't use a traditional socialized medicine system. Instead, it works with private insurers and doctors who accept *la Sécu*'s insurance. You can choose your own doctors and specialists without needing prior approval, avoiding long waiting lists. The system gives people control over their own healthcare while trusting them not to abuse it. Pretty impressive, right?

- **HEALTH**

to feel like a million bucks
avoir une pêche d'enfer

to make it/to hang on
tenir le coup

to not seem like oneself
ne pas être dans son assiette

to get very tired
avoir un coup de pompe/barre

to be dead (tired)
être crevé

to be out of breath/exhausted
être à bout de souffle

She's injured but she's hanging on.
Elle est blessée mais elle tient le coup.

What a long week, I'm dead!
Quelle longue semaine, je suis crevé !

- **TAKING A PISS, A SHIT & OTHER GASSES**

In France, using the bathroom is completely natural and not something people are shy about. If your French host starts talking to you about their digestion in detail, take it as a compliment: you're now part of the family!

shit
merde

the runs
la chiasse

I gotta...
Je dois...

> **pee/take a leak/piss**
> *pisser*
>
> **tinkle**
> *faire pipi*
>
> **poo**
> *faire caca*
>
> **take a dump/shit**
> *chier*
>
> **burp**
> *roter*
>
> **fart**
> *péter*

I peed my pants.
Je me suis pissé dessus.

Jordan is looking for the toilets because he needs to take a dump.
Jordan cherche les toilettes car il doit chier.

Damn! I ate too much cheese and now I have the runs!
Merde ! J'ai mangé trop de fromage et maintenant j'ai la chiasse !

F**k! Who farted? Smells like death!
Putain, qui a pété ? Ça pue la mort !

- **DEATH**

Everyone who loves life is scared of dying. As Woody Allen, beloved by the French, said, "I'm not afraid of death; I just don't want to be there when it happens." Because of this fear, people use ironic or strange terms to talk about death.

to die
claquer

to leave a place in a coffin
sortir les pieds devant

cemetery
boulevard des allongés

to have a brush with death
frôler la mort

to smell like death
sentir le sapin

to be at the end of one's days/to be exhausted
être au bout du rouleau

Smells like death in this house.
Ça sent le sapin dans cette maison.

Marius had an accident, he brushed death!
Marius a eu un accident, il a frôlé la mort !

- **GIVING LIFE**

to take the pill
prendre la pilule

to show (during pregnancy)
avoir le ballon/le gros bide

to have a bun in the oven
avoir un polichinelle dans le tiroir

to be pregnant
être enceinte jusqu'à l'os

Carole is taking the pill to not get pregnant.

Carole prend la pilule pour ne pas tomber enceinte.

You didn't know? She has a bun in the oven!
Tu savais pas ? Elle a un polichinelle dans le tiroir !

- **HURTING**

boo-boo
bobo

ouch!
aïe !

to heal/to get better
s'en sortir

to die of pain
crever de mal

to have a headache
avoir mal au caillou

to be boiling (with fever)
être bouillant (de fièvre)

vegetable
légume

to catch a cold
choper froid
choper la crève

to catch a nasty disease
choper une saloperie

STD
MST (Maladie Sexuellement Transmissible)

AIDS
SIDA (Syndrome d'Immuno Déficience Acquise)

People who are in a coma are vegetables.
Les gens qui sont dans le coma sont des légumes.

Put on a scarf otherwise you'll catch a cold!
Mets une écharpe sinon tu vas attraper la crève !

It's nothing, it's just a small boo-boo.
C'est rien du tout, c'est juste un petit bobo.

- **DOCTORS**

to take some medicine
prendre un médoc

hospital
hosto

doctor
toubib

physical therapist
physio

gyno
gynéco
guigne trou

eye doctor
zieutiste

surgeon
tranche-lard

Hurry up, we need to go to the hospital!
Grouille-toi, faut qu'on aille à l'hosto !

The doc prescribed me some medicine I need to take.
Le toubib m'a prescrit des médocs que je dois prendre.

Caroline caught an eye infection, she needs to go to the eye doctor.
Caroline a chopé une infection à l'œil, elle doit aller chez le zieutiste.

10. Emotion Explosion

French classicism was one of the most influential movements in history. Writers like Jean Racine and Pierre Corneille used ancient Roman and Greek rules to create formal and restrained principles in literature. This movement spread into all areas of French life. However, modern France is not just about reason and high virtues – emotions are very present in daily life. While courage was a key value in classicism, fear, anger, and envy are central to modern slang.

Except for a short period during the German occupation and Vichy government, freedom of expression has always been highly valued in France. The direct and mocking tone in French media is unique, and you'll find that political newspapers and TV shows often present a different image than what the government wants. The saying *toutes les vérités sont bonnes à dire* (all truths are good to tell) reflects this attitude, and humor remains a powerful way to share opinions.

to show off
en mettre plein la vue

se la péter
frimer

to be thrilled
être emballé par qqch

to do really well
cartonner

to be a great success
faire un tabac

to be dying to
crever d'envie

to die of envy
crever de jalousie

um, not really
bof

to not give a damn
en avoir rien à cirer

to not give a shit
en avoir rien à foutre
s'en battre les couilles

fking bad**
nul à chier

piece of crap/shit
merde

I am thrilled to be going to China!
Je suis trop emballée par le fait d'aller en Chine !

Maxime did really well at the exams.
Maxime a cartonné aux examens.

I don't give a shit about your story!

J'en ai rien à foutre de ton histoire !

- **COLORED EMOTIONS**

to be green with envy
être vert(e) de jalousie

to be red with anger
être rouge de rage

to be down in the dumps
broyer du noir

to have dark thoughts
avoir des idées noires

Since Marc failed his exams, he's down in the dumps.
Depuis que Marc a raté ses examens, il broie du noir.

This interaction made me red with anger!
Cette interaction m'a rendue rouge de rage !

- **SCAREDY CAT**

to have goosebumps
avoir la chair de poule

to be scared shitless
avoir la trouille

to scare the living daylights out of someone
foutre la frousse à qqn

Going in the cellar scares me shitless!
Aller dans la cave me fout trop la trouille !

- **THE PISSED OFF FRENCH**

These people…
Ces gens…

They…
Ils/Elles…

    are too much
    me gavent

    get on my nerves
    m'énervent

    get up my ass
    m'emmerdent

    tick me off
    me gonflent

    wear me out
    me saoulent

I can't…
Je peux pas…

    stand you
    te supporter
    te saquer

    put up with them anymore
    les supporter

    stand the sight of him/her
    le/la voir

You are…
Tu es…

    so full of shit

complètement faux cul

out of control
complètement givré(e)

a pain in the ass
chiant(e)

to let out a yell
pousser un coup de gueule/une gueulée

to be in a huff/in a bad mood
tirer la gueule
faire la tête

to be/to get upset
avoir les boules

to wince
tiquer

to grumble/to be grumpy
faire le grognon
être bougon/ grincheux

to sulk
bouder

to make a little mistake
faire une boulette

Jeanne was fired so she's in a bad mood.
Jeanne a été virée donc elle tire la gueule.

Why are you sulking?
Pourquoi tu boudes ?

I think I made a mistake.
Je pense que j'ai fait une boulette.

• THE JOKER FRENCH

joke
blague
vanne

to joke
blaguer

to joke around
rigoler

to have a lot of fun
se marrer

to tell lies
raconter des bobards/salades

to make fun of someone
se foutre
se ficher de la gueule de qqn

to buy (a story)
gober

No need to get angry, I was joking!
Ne te fâche pas, je blaguais !

We have such a good time at the funfair!
On se marre trop à la fête foraine !

I can't believe you bought what he said!
J'arrive pas à croire que tu as gobé ce qu'il a dit !

11. Money, Money, Money

Before the euro, France used the *franc*. But switching to the euro wasn't the first time the French had changed currencies. In 1960, the *franc nouveau* replaced the *franc lourd*, which was then called the *franc ancien*. People had to divide the old price by 100 to get the new one. Many millionaires in *francs lourds* suddenly became just "thousandaires." Like any big change, people were attached to the old ways and found the new currency difficult. Even TV journalists used both values to help people adapt.

On January 1, 1999 France adopted the euro, the collective European Union currency. The change created both fear and excitement. Interestingly, old people who have lived through both monetary changes still refer to the *franc ancien*!

Money has inspired many slang words and popular expressions. Whether loved or despised, cash has left a lasting mark on the French language.

- **CASH**

cash
fric

money
pognon
flouze
thune

dime/coin
rond

buck
balle

I'm out of money!
Je n'ai plus de thune !

It's the end of the month, I don't have a dime.
C'est la fin du mois, je n'ai plus un rond.

This pair of shoes costs seventy-five bucks.
Cette paire de pompes coûte soixante-quinze balles.

- **FOR RICHER OR FOR POORER**

to be stingy/cheap
être radin(e)

to wind up in the poorhouse
finir sur la paille

to be flat broke
être fauché
être à sec

poverty/hardship

dèche

to beg for money
faire la manche

to be in the red
être dans le rouge

to be loaded
être friqué

to fill one's pockets
se remplir les poches

to waste
claquer

to burn
flamber

big spender
flambeur, flambeuse

There are always people begging in the subway.
Y a toujours des gens qui font la manche dans le métro.

The end of the month is always a hardship.
C'est toujours la dèche à la fin du mois.

We've spent too much, we're in the red.
On a trop dépensé, on est dans le rouge.

- **COST OF LIVING**

France is famous for its high taxes. Fortunately, places like Luxembourg, Switzerland, and Monaco are just around the corner and offer tax breaks. Many artists, athletes, CEOs, and big companies have moved to Switzerland or Luxembourg to save money.

In France, people have different attitudes about money: some work to live, while others live to work. Despite the high taxes, many wealthy people still remain, especially around the Champs-Elysées.

to be expensive
douiller

to have discount prices
casser les prix

lowest price
prix plancher

to be cheap
être donné

to cost an arm and a leg
coûter la peau du cul

This t-shirt is not cheap!
Ce t-shirt n'est pas donné !

Your trip to Norway will be very expensive.
Tu vas douiller pendant ton voyage en Norvège.

12. Drinking, Dancing, Puking

Going out in France can take many forms: you might spend a Saturday night at a club, dancing to electronic and techno music until the early morning; or you could relax at an outdoor café, sipping Bordeaux while gazing into the eyes of someone you love. If that's not your style, maybe you'll head to a cabaret or nightclub and chat with the strippers and hookers who hang out there.

Drinking alcohol is a big part of French culture. It's normal to drink wine every day, and even kids are allowed to have some diluted with water. Since France is mainly Catholic, drinking wine, considered the blood of their savior, can be seen as an act of faith.

Ask anyone where the best wine in the world is made, and they'll say France. French wine isn't just for the wealthy anymore; you can find bottles of Beaujolais Nouveau at every 7-Eleven. However, while wine sales are rising in the US, they are dropping in France. Since 2000, wine exports have fallen by 6%, and France has lost over a million wine drinkers – not because of cirrhosis but due to persuasive health campaigns. Older French people miss their wine-filled lunches and hate that beer is becoming the favorite drink for Generations X and Y.

• GOT PLANS TONIGHT?

to go for a drink
aller boire un coup

Do you have plans tonight?
T'as des projets ce soir ?

You goin' out?
Tu sors ?

What're you doin'?
Tu fais quoi ?

Are you busy tonight?
Tu fais quelque chose ce soir ?

I'm bored shitless.
Je me fais chier comme c'est pas possible.

Let's have a drink somewhere.
Allons boire un coup quelque part.

This place sucks.
C'est nul ici.

This place looks dangerous.
Ça craint ici.

Should we go?
On bouge?

Should we get out of here?
On se tire ?

Should we blow this joint?

On se casse ?

Don't be such a buzz kill!
Ne nous casse pas les couilles!

- **NIGHT OUT**

noise
boucan

brothel
bordel

whore/hooker
pute

Can you stop making all that noise?
Vous pouvez arrêter tout ce boucan ?

Is there a brothel around here?
Y a un bordel par ici ?

- **PARTY TIME!**

The French have more words for "party" than the ancient Greeks had gods. They use terms like *la fête, la bringue, la java, la noce, la bomba, la nouba, la bamboche, la bamboula, la fiesta, la teuf, la ribote, la goguette*, and *la ribouldingue*. Some French parties get so wild they make MTV Spring Breaks look like your stepmom's Easter potluck. So get ready by learning these party words.

party
teuf (verlan of fête)

party animal
un fêtard

bouncer

videur

I feel like partying!
Je suis d'humeur à faire la fête !

I'm up for anything.
Je suis prêt(e) à tout.

I wanna have a great time tonight.
Je veux m'éclater ce soir.

I'm gonna let loose!
Je vais me déchaîner !

I'm fed up with beer. Let's go dancing for once.
J'en ai marre de la bière. Allons danser pour une fois.

This place is happenin'.
Ça chauffe ici.

- **LET'S GET DOWN!**

The minimum drinking age in France is eighteen, but no one really cares. If you can see over the counter, you can buy alcohol. The same goes for clubs – if you look good and are dressed well, the bouncer will let you in, no matter your age. Most places stay open all night, so there's no rush to drink quickly once you get to the bar.

Let's do an all-nighter.
Faisons nuit blanche

Want another drink?
Tu veux un autre verre ?

Wanna go home with me?
Tu veux rentrer avec moi ?

Let's…

hit on some guys
branchons des mecs

hit on some girls
branchons des gonzesses/des filles/des nanas

get laid (with a girl)
allons nous taper des gonzesses/des filles/des nanas

- **WHERE YOU AT?**

Bars and pharmacies are the most common businesses that can be found in a typical French city. It's surprising how many pharmacies there are... Could this have to do with France's affordable health care that covers everyone's medication? You tell me!

Let's go to...
Allons...

    a bar/café
    au bistro

    a bar
    un bar

    a bar-tobacco shop
    un bar-tabac

    a café
    un café

    a café-theater
    un café-théâtre

    a music bar
    un café-concert

a cabaret
un cabaret

a nightclub
une boîte de nuit
un night-club

a rave
une rave

the "afters"
l'after

a sandwich hut/trailer/kiosk
une baraque à sandwich
un kiosque à sandwich

a swingers club
un club libertin
une boîte échangiste

a disco
une boîte de nuit
une boîte
une discothèque

- **THE BOOZE**

France's love for wine means you can buy it almost anywhere, even finding great bottles at good prices in supermarkets. It's like buying Dom Pérignon at a 7-Eleven. Avoid the plastic bottles of wine, though – they're cheap for a reason and can make you sick. Beer is more popular in the north and northeast of the country.

Cheers!
Santé !
Tchin-tchin !

To good friends!

Aux amis !

To Napoleon, that midget asshole.
À Napoléon, ce con de nain !

You got beer on tap?
Vous avez des bières à la pression ?

Gimme a...
Donne-moi...

> **beer**
> *de la bière*
>
> **cheap beer**
> *de la bibine*
>
> **glass of beer**
> *un demi*
>
> **pint**
> *une pinte*
>
> **liter of beer**
> *un litre*

Let's pound these shots.
On va se les faire cul sec.

Hey bartender, a round for my friends.
M'sieu, une tournée pour mes amis.

Chug! Chug! Chug!
Eh glou ! Eh glou ! Eh glou !

- **FINE LIKE WINE**

Who's buried in Grant's Tomb? Where does Champagne come from? French wines are named after the region they come from. The most famous reds are

Bordeaux from the southwest and *Bourgogne* from the center. You can also find good, cheaper reds from the Marseille region, like *Côtes du Rhône*.

May I have a glass of...?
Puis-je avoir un verre de...?

red wine
vin rouge

white wine
vin blanc

rosé wine
vin rosé

Champagne/sparkling wine
Champagne

Wine coolers don't exist in France, but there's a drink called a "kir," which is wine mixed with other alcohol. The classic kir is two-thirds white wine (*Bourgogne Aligoté*) and one-third *crème de cassis* (black currant liquor). But there are many variations, and they're all delicious:

I would like a...
Je voudrais un...

Kir normand
Cider with crème de cassis

Kir cardinal
Red Bordeaux with crème de cassis

Kir royal
Champagne with crème de cassis

Kir impérial
Champagne with crème de framboise (raspberry)

Le Double K
The Krushchev Kir (white wine, vodka, crème de cassis)

- **LIQUORS**

Many French people, especially in the countryside, still make their own brandy and cognac. If you're invited for dinner, your host might serve some at the end of the meal from a clear bottle with a handwritten label or no label at all, often with a pear or apricot floating in it. Compared to these homemade spirits, Mezcal tastes like candy. It's considered bad manners to refuse, as it's a tradition to enjoy these drinks with guests.

Around cities, French youth follow the saying *"Blanc sur rouge, rien ne bouge; rouge sur blanc, tout fout le camp,"* which means "White on red, nothing moves; red on white, everything goes." This is similar to the American saying, "Beer before liquor, never been sicker; liquor before beer, you're in the clear." In France, the advice is to start with a light drink and finish with a strong one, the opposite of the American approach.

Pour me...
Versez-moi...

un Pastis
You add a little water and an ice cube to an anis liqueur and the yellowish liqueur turns white. Drink a bunch of these and you'll have a blinding headache like you've never known.

un Panaché
A lemonade beer tastes great, especially when it's hot or in the afternoon.

un Despérado
A beer with tequila in it.

une Eau-de-vie
Brandy

une Poire William
It takes sixty-one pounds of pears to make two liters of this pear brandy!

un Calvados
Apple brandy from Normandy.

un Trou Normand
This Calvados-type drink, which translates to "The Norman Hole," is a killer. After

a really heavy meal, you're supposed to throw this burning mixture down the hatch in order to sear a hole through your just-digested food and make room for dessert.

- ## **LET'S GET WASTED**

By the time you use the expressions in this section, it'll probably already be too late.

to get plastered
se déchirer

to get drunk
se prendre une torchée
se saouler (la gueule)
se prendre une cuite

I'm starting to get…
Je commence à être…

> **a little tipsy**
> *un peu pompette*
>
> **buzzed**
> *bourré(e)*
>
> **sick**
> *malade*

That dumb tourist is…
Ce con de touriste est…

> **smashed**
> *fracassé(e)*
>
> **really trashed**
> *complètement défoncé(e)*
>
> **three sheets to the wind**
> *complètement dans les vapes*

complètement à l'ouest

about to puke
sur le point de gerber/dégueuler/déballer

I'm gonna get ripped!
Je vais me fracasser!

She's really lit!
Elle est complètement allumée !

We're so fucked up!
On est complètement défoncés !

Your dad is an alcoholic.
Ton père est alcoolo.

She is going to become a drunkard!
Elle va devenir ivrogne !

- **SLOWING DOWN**

After a few nights of non-stop partying in Nice or Lyon, you'll be happy to know these phrases:

to have a hangover
avoir la tête dans le cul
avoir la gueule de bois

Tonight I…
Ce soir je…

> **am toast**
> *suis crevé(e)*
>
> **am going home early**
> *vais rentrer tôt*
>
> **wanna catch a flick**

veux me faire un cinoche

am gonna kick back
vais me la filer tranquille

am gonna chill out
vais me la couler douce

am just hangin' out at home
traine a la maison

am not gonna do squat
vais rien foutre
vais glander

am gonna just jack around
vais branler que dalle

to go to bed
se pieuter

to sleep
pioncer

to sleep over/to crash
pioncer chez qqn

to sleep in
faire la grasse matinée

Tomorrow is the weekend, we'll be able to not do squat.
Demain c'est le week-end, on va pouvoir glander.

It's late, time to go to bed.
Il est tard, temps de pioncer.

On Sundays, I sleep in.
Les dimanches, je fais la grasse matinée.

13. Looking for Trouble, Keeping the Peace

The US and France have very different attitudes toward war. France, once known for its warriors – think of a certain small man named Napoléon – now prefers peace and diplomacy. For refusing to join the coalition against Iraq and other conflicts, French products actually were boycotted in the US, where some Americans stopped buying Camembert and Bordeaux until France changed its stance.

If the Iraq war had been short, the French might have understood the boycott. But after five years, most French people don't agree. Try taking away a French person's favorite cheese and wine for that long, and you'll see why tensions might rise!

Today, conflicts in France usually revolve around food, drink, sports, politics, and the police. To avoid arguments, use polite expressions and body language. With the right approach, you can save yourself from unnecessary trouble and costly medical bills.

- **ANNOYANCES**

to make something more complicated
chercher midi à quatorze heures

to be looking for trouble
chercher qqn

to ask for trouble
chercher la petite bête

to look for a fight
chercher la baston

to really annoy
pomper l'air

to break someone's balls
casser les couilles

to annoy someone/to piss someone off
faire chier qqn

to be bored
se faire chier

Stop complicating things, you're making your life harder!
Arrête de chercher midi à quatorze heures, tu te compliques la vie !

Stop it with your bullshit, you're pissing me off!
Arrête tes conneries, tu me fais chier !

Don't make that face, you were looking for trouble!
Fais pas cette tête, tu l'as cherché !

- **INTERJECTIONS**

crap

mince
zut

shit
merde

Merde can be used in almost any situation. Whether you lose your keys, forget something important, or are annoyed with someone, *merde* is your best bud.

f**k
putain
bordel

that sucks / what a bummer
ça fait chier

f**kin'
saloperie (de bordel de merde)

f**k / goddamn it
putain de bordel de merde

This is a vulgar expression whose meaning is clear from its literal translation. It comes from a story about an unknown poet who often frequented a *putain de bordel*, a brothel whore, who threw the contents of her chamber pot in his face. While there is no exact English equivalent to this expression, the closest translation is f**k!

Crap, I forgot my wallet!
Mince, j'ai oublié mon portefeuille !

The pharmacy is closed, that sucks!
Fait chier, la pharmacie est fermée !

- **INSULTS**

The French are experts at insulting, way ahead of other Europeans. Their fiery Latin blood mixed with Celtic barbarian roots creates a dual temperament that not only enjoys insulting but has turned it into an art. They often string together multiple insults in one go. However, the trick is to insult subtly so that if questioned, the remarks can seem perfectly fine.

You..
Espèce de..

> **dirty**
> *sale*
>
> **f**king son of a bitch!**
> *sacré fils de pute !*
>
> **dickhead**
> *salopard*
>
> **f**ker**
> *salaud*
>
> **fat**
> *gros, grosse*
>
> **small**
> *p'tit, p'tite*

Stop driving in the middle, you dickhead!
Arrête de conduire au milieu, espèce de salopard !

You broke my phone you asshole !
T'as cassé mon téléphone espèce d'enfoiré !

Your friend is really a fat jerk.
Ton pote est vraiment un gros con.

- **NASTIER INSULTS**

asshole/f**khead
enfoiré(e)
enculé(e)

jerk/idiot
con

dickhead
tête de con

asshole/cunt
connard (guy)

bitch
connasse

bastard
bâtard(e)

wimp
lavette
mauviette

Mauviette and *lavette* refer exclusively to weak, fearful men. Using the feminine article makes the insult that much stronger, implying they aren't real men at all.

coward
couille molle

bitch
salope

He almost ran me over, what an asshole!
Il a failli me renverser, quel connard !

You're a real f**ker!
T'es un vrai salaud toi !

Go f**k yourself bastard!
Va te faire foutre bâtard !

- **ORIGINS**

France isn't as sensitive about race as the US. Race talk can upset people, but not as much as it does in America.

f**k your race
nique ta race

typical ethnic bastard
enculé de ta race

Instead of race, anything with "mother" in it is gonna get French dudes really pissed off.

motherfucker
enculé de ta mère

f**k your mother
nique ta mère

your mother's a whore
ta mère la pute

son-of-a-bitch
fils de pute

Why you lookin' at me motherfucker?
Qu'est-ce t'as à me regarder, enculé de ta mère ?

F**k you, you son of a bitch!
Nique ta mère espèce de fils de pute !

- **PEACEKEEPING**

to shut up
la fermer
fermer sa gueule

to leave

se casser
se tirer
se tailler

to get out/to take off
se barrer
foutre le camp
bouger

to mind one's own business
s'occuper de ses oignons

to butt in
ramener sa fraise

to shove it
se mettre qqch où je pense

to take a hike
aller se faire voir

to go f**k oneself
aller se faire foutre

chill out
calme-toi

nevermind
laisse tomber

to get over it
tourner la page

to not give a shit
s'en battre les couilles

to leave someone in peace
ficher/foutre la paix à qqn

to call the cops
appeler les flics

No one wants to hear your stories, shut it!
Personne veut entendre tes histoires, ferme-la !

Stop staring at us and mind your own business.
Arrête de nous regarder et occupe-toi de tes oignons.

Let's get out of here, it's too chaotic!
Barrons-nous, c'est trop chaotique !

I don't give a shit about your excuse!
Je m'en bats les couilles de ton excuse !

- **FIGHTING**

to have a problem
avoir un problème

to shout at someone/to scold someone
engueuler qqn

to kick
casser la gueule à qqn

to beat someone black and blue
rouer de coups qqn

to beat the shit out of someone
passer à tabac qqn
tabasser

fight
baston

slap
claque

to fall unconscious
tomber dans les pommes

head-butt
coup de boule

To kick someone in...
Mettre un coup de pied dans...

> **the head**
> *la tête*
>
> **the stomach**
> *le ventre*
>
> **the butt**
> *le cul*

Why are you looking at me, you got a problem?
Pourquoi tu me regardes, t'as un problème ?

I got scolded by my parents.
Je me suis faite engueuler par mes parents.

Martine's boyfriend was beat up.
Le copain de Martine s'est fait tabasser.

- **GETTING ARRESTED**

I won't say a word.
Je dirais rien.

It wasn't me.
C'est pas moi.

I don't know anything.
Je sais rien.

Acting like you don't know shit.
Faire comme si de rien n'était.

I hate you.

Je te déteste.

Get lost.
Fous le camp.

Scram.
Dégage.

Go to hell.
Va te faire voir.

Leave me the hell alone.
Fous-moi la paix.

Fuck off.
Va te faire foutre.

Mr. officer, please, I don't know anything.
Monsieur le policier, s'il vous plaît, je sais rien.

Scram, you'll get caught by the cops!
Dégage, tu vas te faire choper par les keufs !

The cops ended up leaving me alone.
Les flics ont fini par me foutre la paix.

14. Love Language

The French are known as the world's best lovers, and they take great pride in this title. But it's not just their lovemaking skills that earn them this reputation – it's the heartfelt conversations, romantic gestures like giving flowers, and writing love letters and sweet poetry. It's the charm beyond the bedroom that sets them apart.

You'll love the cute nicknames French lovers give each other, ranging from vegetables to flowers and everything in between. They say love has reasons that reason doesn't know. In this spirit, you can call your partner any name sweetly, and it will be endearing. Even words that might seem insulting in other contexts can be charming in France. Would you mind if your *chéri* called you a dog or a rat? In France, it would earn you big points!

You can easily nickname an enemy or call a child *mon petit bonhomme* without issues, but giving a nickname to someone you care about shows intimacy. Being called sweetie, angel, or honey by someone you just met would feel meaningless.

The French believe that nicknames express the bond and closeness between two people.

To enjoy your trip to France and connect with the locals, keep in mind a few cultural differences. Accepting a dinner invitation doesn't necessarily mean sex afterward; a cozy restaurant is more romantic than a crowded pub or noisy disco; the third date rule doesn't apply in France, and a first-date kiss isn't always expected. Your date might just want to get to know you better over dinner, so don't be upset if they don't follow you to your room or hesitate to kiss you; it's just a cultural difference!

- **FALLING**

to like / to have a crush
kiffer

to wink at someone
faire un clin d'œil à qqn

love at first sight
coup de foudre

to catch someone's eye
taper dans l'œil de qqn

to fall for someone
faire craquer qqn

to not resist someone
craquer pour qqn

to be crazy about someone / something
être fou de qqn/qqch

Don't tell anyone: Jeanne has a crush on Martin!
Tu le dis à personne : Jeanne a un kiffe sur Martin !

The day I met my wife, it was love at first sight.
Le jour où j'ai rencontré ma femme, c'était le coup de foudre.

Jonathan is crazy about Camille!
Jonathan est fou de Camille !

- **WOOING**

to tease
allumer

teaser
allumeur, allumeuse

to flirt
flirter
draguer

flirt
dragueur, dragueuse

to sweet-talk/to chat up
baratiner

smooth talker
baratineur, baratineuse

to chase someone
courir après qqn

to have a date
avoir un rencard

Maxime is trying so hard to flirt with you!
Maxime essaie trop de te draguer !

I can't come tonight, I have a date.
Je ne peux pas venir ce soir, j'ai un rencard.

The guy at the bar, avoid him, he's a smooth talker.
Le gars au bar, évitez-le, c'est un baratineur.

- **THE FRENCH TOUCH**

When intimate, French partners call each other all kinds of sweet, strange, and unexpected names. Those creative souls will use the most uncommon sweet nicknames, taking inspiration from animals and even vegetables.

my love
mon amour

my heart
mon cœur

my fatty one
mon p'tit grassouillet

my ladybug
ma coccinelle

chicken
poussin

my wolf
mon loulou

my cabbage
mon chou

my sugar
mon sucre

Everything sounds sweeter when *en sucre* (of sugar) or *d'amour* (of love) is added, like *mon lapin en sucre* or *mon lapin d'amour*.

Good morning my heart of love, did you sleep well?
Bonjour mon cœur d'amour, tu as bien dormi ?

Did you have a good day, my cabbage?
T'as passé une bonne journée, mon chou ?

- **THE HONEYMOON PHASE**

to see life through rose-colored glasses
voir la vie en rose

to be on cloud nine
être sur un petit nuage

cuddle/hug
câlin

to hug/to cuddle
câliner

to caress
caresser
donner une caresse

hickey
suçon

to tickle
chatouiller
faire des chatouilles

Since he got a new girlfriend, Félix's been on cloud nine.
Depuis qu'il a une nouvelle copine, Félix est sur son petit nuage.

Clara, what's that hickey?
Clara, c'est quoi ce suçon ?

I love cuddling with my girlfriend.
J'adore câliner ma copine.

- **BUMPS IN THE ROAD**

to stand someone up
poser un lapin

to be rejected
se prendre un râteau

to cheat on someone
tromper qqn

cuckold (man who is cheated on)
cocu

The guy I was supposed to meet stood me up.
Le mec que je devais retrouver m'a posé un lapin.

Quentin cheated on Marie; she's devastated.
Quentin a trompé Marie ; elle est dévastée.

- **IT'S OVER**

to dump someone
plaquer qqn
larguer qqn

to break up
rompre

the break up
la rupture

to blow someone off
envoyer balader qqn

to send away
envoyer chier

to turn the page
tourner la page

I got dumped by Maxime.
Je me suis faite plaquer par Maxime.

It's been five months since we broke up, it's time to turn the page.
Ça fait cinq mois qu'on a rompu, il est temps de tourner la page.

- **NEW BEGINNINGS**

to get back together
se remettre ensemble

to glue the pieces back together
recoller les morceaux

Jacques and I have decided to get back together.
Jacques et moi avons décidé de nous remettre ensemble.

15. Intercourse

French cultural traditions can be stronger than their motto of *liberté, égalité, fraternité*. Men are given some leeway to pursue women, often seen as a natural urge. A man who chases many women is called a *coureur de jupons* (skirt chaser), but a woman who dates many men is labeled *une pute* (a whore). Meanwhile, women who are hard to win over are also criticized – a classic case of "damned if they do, damned if they don't."

uptight
coincé(e) du bulbe

to check someone out
mater qqn

to get an eyeful
se rincer l'œil

to be sex starved
être en manque (de sexe)

sex
baise

f**kable
baisable

f**k
baiseur, baiseuse

good/bad in bed
bon/mauvais au pieu

horndog (guy who sleeps around)
chaud lapin

casanova
casanova
don juan

skirt-chaser
coureur de jupons

hottie
chaudasse

prostitute/whore
traînée
pute

man-eater
mangeuse d'hommes

Kevin is tense, he's sex-starved.
Kevin est tendu, il est en manque de baise.

Dude, check out this hottie, she's so f**kable!
Mec, check cette chaudasse, elle est trop baisable !

Alexandre flirts with everyone, he's such a Casanova.
Alexandre drague toutes les meufs, c'est vraiment un Casanova.

- **SEXUAL ORIENTATION**

Homosexual slang changes with time. *La (grande) folle* (the queer, literally "the (big) crazy woman") became popular after the French-Italian movie *La Cage aux Folles* (1978). This film humorously portrayed effeminate men dressing and acting like women. After thirty years, the term *la (grande) folle* is outdated. Now, the most common terms are *homo* and *gay*, followed by *PD* or *pédé*, short for *pédéraste* (from the ancient Greek model of sexuality, which was men with teenagers). Another term, *la pédale*, was popularized by the movie *Pédale Douce* (Sweet Gay), and finally *la tapette* (gay, literally "little hit/kick") is also used, implying a lack of strength and masculinity.

bi
bi

tranny/transvestite
travelo

to be gay/lesbian
être de l'autre bord

to change sides/teams
virer de bord

to be gay
être pd (pédé)

lesbian
gouine

I need to tell you something; I'm bi.
Faut que je vous dise quelque chose ; je suis bi.

After his divorce from Amélie, Thomas changed teams. He's got a boyfriend now!
Après son divorce d'Amélie, Thomas a viré de bord. Il a un copain maintenant !

Did you know that our math professor is gay?
Tu sais que notre prof de maths est pédé ?

- **SEXY BODY PARTS**

The French have so many words for genitals that they could fill a small dictionary – which makes sense given the popularity of this conversation topic!

ass
cul
croupe

asshole
trou du cul/de balle

Many Frenchmen call their reproductive organs *bijoux de famille* (family jewels) or *bourse* (purse). DIY enthusiasts might compare them to tools like *le chalumeau* (welding torch), *le tuyau d'arrosage* (hosepipe), or *gaule* (pole). Those looking for a quickie might refer to them as a *levier de vitesse* (gear stick), while hungry others might compare them to food items like an *asperge* (asparagus), *baguette*, *carotte*, a *friandise* (delicacy), *sucre d'orge* (rock candy), or an *os à moelle* (marrow bone)...

dick
bite
queue
grand chauve à col roulé

wiener
saucisse

pecker
quéquette

wee-wee
zizi

balls
couilles
roubignoles

nuts
bonbons

French slang has been influenced by female organs too. While "cunt" is a vulgar term in English, the French prefer to use more positive words for the vagina.

pussy
chatte
foufoune
minet

pussy lips
lèvres

bush
touffe

tits
seins
nichons

titties
les tétés

nipples
mamelons

rack
balcon

buttocks
miches

Seeing your ass gives me a hard on.
Voir ton cul me fait trop bander.

Keep your dick in your pants!
Garde ta bite dans ton pantalon !

I really need to shave my bush before my date!
Faut absolument que je me rase la touffe avant mon rencard !

Justin said he wanted to kiss my lips, but he wasn't talking about my mouth.
Justin a dit qu'il voulait embrasser mes lèvres, mais il ne parlait pas de ma bouche.

- **TOOLS**

condom
capote
préservatif

dildo
godemichet

vibrator
vibro

We were planning to have sex and you didn't bring any condoms? You dickhead!
On a prévu de baiser et tu n'as pas amené de capotes ? Espèce de con !

- **HEATING UP**

to get a hard-on
bander

to get soft
débander

hard-on
barreau

to get wet
mouiller

wet
mouillé(e)

to masturbate
se branler

to finger
doigter

jerking off
branlette

to turn someone on
exciter qqn

Camille is so hot, she gives me a hard-on.
Camille est trop bonne, elle me donne le barreau.

Stop masturbating all day, you're disgusting!
Arrête de te branler toute la journée, t'es dégueulasse !

Mathias prefers jerking off to sex.
Mathias préfère la branlette à la baise.

Stop turning me on, we're at the restaurant!
Arrête de m'exciter, on est au resto !

- **FIRST, SECOND AND THIRD BASE**

The French are known for being great lovers, but it's not because they're physically better equipped for it. On the contrary, they just have more time for sex thanks to their shorter workweeks and five weeks of vacation each year!

to French-kiss someone / to make out with someone
rouler une pelle à qqn

to feel someone up
peloter

to give a blowjob
tailler une pipe à qqn

cunnilingus
lécher la chatte

roll between the sheets
partie de jambes en l'air

to f**k somebody
se taper qqn

to do someone
se faire qqn

Let's…
Allons…

    f**k/screw
    baiser
    niquer
    coucher

    fornicate
    forniquer

    make love
    faire l'amour

    sleep together
    coucher ensemble

    fuck like rabbits
    baiser comme des lapins

    have a quickie
    tirer un coup rapidos

to take someone from the front/behind
prendre par devant/derrière

to bend over
se cambrer

orgy
partouze

suck
sucer

naughty thing(s)
cochonnerie(s)

to heat up/to cool off
faire monter/descendre la température

seventh heaven
septième ciel

to come
jouir

cum
foutre

sperm
sperme

Manon and Dylan made out at the party!
Manon et Dylan se sont roulés une pelle à la teuf!

He asked me to give him a blowjob.
Il m'a demandé de lui tailler une pipe.

My friend f**ked a girl in the bathroom.
Mon pote s'est tapé une meuf dans les chiottes.

Chris told me that he wants to do so many naughty things with me.
Chris m'a dit qu'il a envie de faire plein de cochonneries avec moi.

I came and ended up in seventh heaven.
J'ai jouis et je me suis retrouvée au septième ciel.

Download the Audiobook & PDF below!

www.ingramcontent.com/pod-product-compliance
Lightning Source LLC
LaVergne TN
LVHW051916060526
838200LV00004B/171